DEAR MARGO,

HERE'S TO LEAVING OUR FUNK

AT THE DOOR AND HAVING A

GREAT DAY EVERYDAY.

Thanks for being my

friend.

Love

Stevie

Leave Your Funk at the Door

Customer Service Is Not About the Customer

Steve Beck

BCK Publications
Chicago, IL

FIRST EDITION

ISBN No. 978-0-9832008-1-9

Leave Your Funk at the Door is available at special
quantity discounts to use as premiums, or for use in
corporate training programs. For more information,
please send inquiries to stevebeck@beckseminars.com

This book is dedicated to
my beautiful wife Kim who is
my greatest supporter.

TABLE OF CONTENTS

ACKNOWLEDGMENTS

To Ole Larsen (my teacher) who taught me many, many lessons, especially to WAKE UP!

To my parents, Richard and Louise Beck, who taught me the importance of treating others with respect.

To Susan McBride for her brilliant editing.

To Stephanie Beck my daughter for her wonderful support and editing skills.

To Richard and Katie Beck my other two wonderful children who add so much Love to my life.

To the tens of thousands of people who have attended my seminars, for generously sharing their experiences and their willingness to explore ways they can improve their lives.

To John Brandt my friend and teacher who has shared and taught me a whole lot about sales, marketing, and customer service.

To all of my Customers who have hired me to 'Fire Up' their staff…Thank you!

To Jeff and Val Gee who explained the concept that 'Everyone is your Customer'.

To Emily Petroff who epitomizes customer service in everything she does.

To Leonard Vance for help editing the book.

To Ryan Elliot who always makes things simple and easy so I believe I can accomplish it.

To Dan White who is my webmaster, friend, and advisor for all of his wisdom.

Special Thanks

To my friend and writing partner,
Leslie Lindeman,
without whose contribution this book
would not be all that it is.

I was standing in the middle of the grocery store like a lost child. I couldn't find the taco seasoning. Outside, it was pouring, and I was running late.

I'm not great in large grocery stores, or at least I wasn't until this day. They're huge and mysterious and nothing is ever where it seems it should be. Mayonnaise goes on sandwiches, so shouldn't the mayo be next to the bread? It never is.

I walked all over the store looking for the taco seasoning. I thought it would be by the taco shells, but it wasn't. By the ground beef? Not even close. Near the pinto beans? No.

I asked an older woman who looked like she'd been shopping in this store half her life, "Do you know where the taco seasoning is?"

She barely lifted her eyes from a box of spaghetti. "I've never made tacos in my life," she said.

Just then a man walked by. He was in a shirt and tie, and hurrying, but I blurted, "Where is the taco seasoning!?"

He immediately stopped. He turned and gave me his full attention. I saw from his nametag that he was the assistant manager. There's a 50-50 chance he'll know where it is, I thought. He'll point and guess, like they do in most grocery stores, or he'll summon a lower-level employee, who will send me back to the aisle with the taco shells and I'll have wasted five more minutes.

"Can I help you?" he said.

"I'm looking for the taco seasoning," I said.

"That's in aisle 4," he said, "between the condiments and the spices."

Then, as I looked up at the signs—we were standing at the end of aisle 11—he said, "Let me show you where that is"

Impossible, I thought. It was rush hour and the store was jammed. There was no way the assistant manager was going to drop everything and accompany a man who wasn't pushing a cart, wasn't even carrying a basket, on his ill-fated mission to find a one dollar and forty-nine cent item.

But that's exactly what he did.

That was "one."

In the "15 Items or Less" line, the checker looked me in the eye and smiled. It wasn't a cheap, cheesy, absent-minded, I'm-supposed-to-look-like-I'm-smiling, smile. She really smiled at me. *At me.* Then she said, "I'm sorry it's raining sir," and I realized she was noticing I didn't have a raincoat or an umbrella. I was in a hurry, but her concern was so real it stopped me for a moment. I looked at her like I was seeing a cashier for the first time. She really was sorry.

That was "two."

The woman bagging the groceries — my six packets of taco seasoning — looked like she was about 65 years old and she was smiling at me so broadly I couldn't miss the fact that she had a couple of teeth missing. She was wearing a raincoat and hat, and she had an umbrella. "May I help you out to the car today, sir?" she said.

I should point out that I am 6 feet 2 inches tall and pretty fit. Even if I had a dozen 20-pound bags of ice and was walking out into a hurricane, I could make it to the car without the aid of a lady old enough to be my mom. But she meant it, and she was ready to go.

I fell in love with that woman. I wanted to put her in my pocket and take her home. Her concern for me, like that of the cashier, was so genuine, I felt as if they loved me. That was "three."

We all are skeptical when we walk into a situation where we are the customer being served by someone representing a business. "They must be doing it for the money," we tell ourselves or because their bosses are all over them. Or for a tip. We live in a fast-paced, often impersonal world, and it's hard to get through our defenses.

But that rainy evening in the Dominick's grocery store not far from my home outside Chicago, those three people broke down my walls. They turned them into rubble with authentic kindness and their desire to go beyond just helping me get what I came for. They wanted me to have an exceptional experience and they succeeded.

11

In that moment, as I walked out into the rain, as happy as a kid on Christmas morning, I became a loyal Dominick's customer. I go there at least a couple of times a week and have for over 12 years. I drive past other grocery stores to get there. I can't remember the last time I was in another grocery store.

I think of the store as *my* Dominick's. I am so loyal I feel like part of their team. Everyone knows the competition in Chicago between Dominick's and rivals is fierce. I feel so strongly about my store that I want *my* Dominick's to win. Their pride is my pride. I pick up litter in the parking lot, I sometimes push stray grocery carts back into the corral, and I'm so familiar with the store now that I can share with my fellow customers where to find just about anything.

Was my incredible three-part experience that rainy evening just a stroke of incredible luck for the store? I don't think so. No matter who the cashier is, when they swipe my card they say, "Thank you, Mr. Beck." EVERY TIME!

The grocery baggers ask me if I would like help out to my car. EVERY TIME! It's the way they *say* it too! They say it as though they really *want* to serve me, not as though I'm a lazy dog or a weakling. It comes from *wanting* to serve me. Their motivation is not a desire to look good or to be seen in a certain way. They really do want to serve me. They aren't pretending.

It's important to note that the experience felt so good, I told myself that I would come back to Dominick's the next time just to see if they could repeat their performance. They did over and over again even at different Dominick's in the Chicagoland area. My daughter's traveling softball team would play in many suburbs of Chicago, so I had the opportunity to visit several Dominick's and they passed with flying colors every time. At some point in that process I decided to only go to Dominick's for our groceries and pledged myself to their place of business.

I continue to be a loyal customer. If one of Dominick's competitors offered me free bread or free milk, I wouldn't switch grocery stores.

I'm so loyal to my Dominick's I'm writing a book about them.

OK, this book isn't actually about Dominick's, but it is about what I call, "creating Customer Loyalty by delivering Exceptional Customer Service or "ECS," pronounced "X." The difference between you and your competition is how you treat your customers and if you are better at the ECS (X) Factor, you will win that customer's attention and loyalty, as Dominick's did mine.

A 5% increase in Customer Loyalty can increase profitability 25% – 80%.

—HARVARD BUSINESS SCHOOL

CHAPTER ONE

MINING GOLD, CREATING DIAMONDS

Practicing Exceptional Customer Service (ECS) will help you create satisfied customers, which will lead to 'Customer Loyalty.' Customer Loyalty is so important you could say, "It's worth its weight in gold."

Everyone knows gold is valuable. People have been adorning themselves with gold for thousands of years. As this is being written, gold is worth almost $2,000 per ounce.

If you deliver ECS to your satisfied customers, eventually you will break through, the way the Dominick's staff did with me that rainy evening, and you will create Customer Loyalty.

Now, how important is that? Let's examine a statement from Harvard Business School, "A 5% increase in Customer Loyalty can increase profitability 25%-80%."

When you break down the walls of resistance the way the Dominick's staff did with me, what happens is you've made an emotional connection with your customer. This emotional connection creates a response in your customer. In becoming loyal versus simply satisfied, a customer makes a pledge to your business that he or she will come back again.

That's a normal human response. When an experience makes us feel good, we want to repeat it. When I walked out of Dominick's and into the rain that night, I had had an emotional experience. I was now a loyal customer.

A customer who is "emotionally connected" to your place of business is likely to spend 46% more money than a customer who is satisfied but not emotionally bonded.

—GALLOP POLL

Customer satisfaction is like gold, but customer loyalty is like diamonds.

It's not easy to create a diamond. It takes so much pressure to form a diamond that they are created nearly 100 miles beneath the earth's surface over a period of millions of years. It is an extraordinary process that eventually brings them to the surface where they can finally be found.

You may not be able to create a loyal customer with every interaction. Neither the assistant manager nor the cashier got through to me, even though their performances were letter perfect. It took the third instance, the older bagger with her wet umbrella, to finally break through and make that emotional connection.

You don't know when or where or how your delivery of ECS will create a loyal customer. In his landmark book, *Moments of Truth*, former Scandinavian Airlines System (SAS) president Jan Carlzon wrote about brief instances where customers are either won or lost.

When Carlzon took over the airline, it was losing money so he instituted a survey to ask customers what was going on. What his customers told him was during a brief encounter with an employee of the company, usually no longer than 15 seconds, the customer walked away with a positive or negative view of the company. Carlzon coined these brief interactions, "Moments of Truth," and he dedicated himself to making sure his employees where empowered and educated to make these moments as powerful and beneficial for his customers as possible.

Creating customer loyalty depends on you. It depends on you delivering ECS every time you have an interaction with a customer, every time you find yourself in a moment of truth.

What Carlzon also learned is that customers are perceptive, because within 3 to 4 seconds they know the truth.

- They know whether or not you are really there for them.

- They know whether your stated desire to serve them is authentic or phony.

- And they know whether or not they can trust you.

This is another way of saying they know whether or not you really care about them. In a moment, I'll explain where that caring for customers comes from and how this book will teach you to access it no matter how you happen to be feeling, no matter what kind of mood you are in on any given day.

But first, let's consider this question: How important are satisfied customers?

We already know that consistently creating satisfied

customers gets us on the road to creating loyal customers. But there is something else, and it has to do with our changing times.

Research shows that out of 25 dissatisfied customers:

- One customer complains.

- 24 are dissatisfied but don't complain.

- Six of the 24 have "serious" problems.

- The 24 non-complainers tell between 10 and 20 other people about their bad experiences.

Technology is changing so fast that all of the best research available having to do with customers spreading their experiences with your business is constantly being redone. Web sites that let customers write and post "reviews" and that are read by tens of thousands of people, social networking sites, and the ability to send texts and/or use Twitter, are revolutionizing the landscape of what we've traditionally called "word of mouth."

It's impossible to calculate the positive value of a loyal customer or the negative value of a dissatisfied customer. But we know that value is more important than ever before.

That quiet customer who discreetly walks away having suffered an unsatisfactory moment of truth becomes a time bomb in your business waiting to go off. If you stop caring about the customer, the customer will stop caring about you.

—STEVE BECK

I'm Your Customer Who Never Comes Back

I'm a nice customer. All the merchants know me. I'm the one who never complains no matter what kind of service I get.

When I go to a store to buy something, I don't throw my weight around. I try to be thoughtful of the other person. If I get a snobby clerk who gets annoyed because I want to look at several things before I make up my mind, I'm as polite as can be; I don't believe rudeness in return is the answer.

I never complain or criticize, and I wouldn't dream of making a scene in public places as I've witnessed other people do. No, I'm a nice customer, but I'm also the nice customer who never comes back.

That's my little revenge for being abused and taking whatever you hand out, because I know I'm not coming back. This decision doesn't immediately relieve my feelings, but in the long run it's far more satisfying than blowing my top.

A nice customer like me, multiplied by others of my kind, can ruin a business. And there are a lot of nice people like me. When we get pushed far enough, we go to another store where we are appreciated. "He who laughs last," they say, "laughs best." I laugh when I see you frantically advertising to get me back, when you could have kept me in the first place with a few kind words and a smile.

Your business might be in a different town and your situation might be "different," but if business is bad, chances are good that if you changed your attitude the word would get around and I'd change from the nice customer who never comes back to the nice customer who always comes back, and brings his friends.

— ANONYMOUS

This picture of this guy shouting at the top of his lungs represents what happens when someone walks away from your business having had an exceptional experience that makes them want to tell the entire world.

Right now, more than at any time in history, this guy has the means to tell thousands of people about your business. Even though he is a perfectly ordinary person, he has the ability to influence a very large number of potential customers.

We'll get into it in much greater detail in Chapter Three, but I want to end this chapter by telling you a life-changing secret that comes from creating loyal customers. Here it is, THE ONE WHO BENEFITS MOST FROM CREATING LOYAL CUSTOMERS IS…YOU!

Customer service books often focus on all the ways you could and should take care of the customer. For instance, you should look them in the eye, you should always be polite, you should tell them how much you empathize if they are not having a good experience.

This book includes that and goes much further. My main concern is not necessarily the customer; my main concern is you. Why? Because you are the one who takes care of the customer; or doesn't, and therefore everything hinges on **you.** If you are not properly cared for first and foremost, the customer's experience is doomed.

Yes, when you provide Exceptional Customer Service, the customer benefits, your employer benefits, your vendors benefit, and your fellow employees benefit.

But the one who benefits most from your outstanding performance is you. My intent is make you aware of that fact, and to support you in getting great enjoyment from your work and your life by doing a great job. Once you begin to do a fabulous job every day, you will experience some of the greatest satisfaction you can get from life.

Perhaps the greatest truth contained in these pages is that **you** create your own happiness. **You** are the author of your own story, and **you** decide whether that story makes you just a little bit happy, mostly happy or absolutely ecstatic every day. **You** write the story of

LEAVE YOUR FUNK AT THE DOOR

WHAT'S THE BIG DEAL?

- "But I'm not in Customer Service, so...what's the big deal?"

- "I never deal with the end user; why should I care about Customer Service?"

- "I don't have direct contact with the actual customer, so Customer Service really doesn't apply to me."

- "As a supervisor I manage people who touch the customer directly, but I don't."

- "I work the back office/the night shift/ behind the scenes/ in accounting/the warehouse/as a janitor, why should I attend a Customer Service training session?"

If you are asking yourself, "Why all this emphasis on customer service if I don't directly deal with the customer?" Or you're saying, "I'm not in the sales department: they are the ones who really should be great at serving the customer," you're not alone. This concern comes up often in my customer service seminars.

When this issue comes up I turn it around on the group: "How many of you are in sales?" I ask. Some hands go up. I ask again, "How many of you are sales people? Ask yourself, 'Am I a sales person?'"

your life, so here's my suggestion: Write your story. So that YOU ARE THE BIG WINNER!

Pretend that everyone you come into contact with is your customer. Yes, EVERYONE. Your family, friends, partner, spouse, co-workers, neighbors, check out person, waitress and even strangers. When you have an interaction with anyone in your life, give them the benefit of the doubt and treat them like they could be or are great customers. How do you treat the customers you like? I'm guessing with a smile, your full attention, a tone of respect and the point of view that it is a pleasure to serve them. That is only possible when you take care of yourself first. You see, it all begins with you. You are Customer #1. How you take care of yourself determines your readiness to serve everyone else you come in contact with all day long.

Like Customer Loyalty, diamonds are rare and amazing things. The only thing more attractive or more valuable than the diamond itself, is the person capable of creating it. That person is you.

I can tell you right now, 20% of the people who read this book will answer, "I am. I'm a sales person." If I'm working with 100 customer service people, 20 hands will go up. And if I'm working with five customer service people, one will say he or she is in sales.

Here's the reality.

We are ALL Salespeople.

If you check people out, handle orders and troubleshoot over the phone, manage a hardware store, are a pharmacist, a valet who parks cars, or a bellman in a fancy hotel, then you are in sales. I understand, you might not be the one responsible for making the 'sale', but we are all part of the sales team. The better we do, the more effective we are at connecting with the customer, the more "sales" will be made, and one way or another, that benefits everyone.

The opposite is also true. When we fail to connect with the customer, or do less than we could to provide the best experience, the bottom line is affected. Whether we can see it or not, whether we feel it, recognize it or even want to admit it, the service the customer receives, and how he or she feels about the experience, drives everything, especially sales.

You never know what 'making a connection with a customer' will lead to. There are sales trainings, books and CDs on "Relationship Selling." Sales has been and always will be relationship selling. The customer has a relationship with everyone he or she has an interaction with during the sales process, and that customer is assessing whether they like or don't like the service during every one of those interactions. Know that if you are dealing with any customer at any time, you are on stage, so work toward winning an award for customer service, whether you are in sales or not. (This is also true for a website. How friendly and easily accessible products are is a sign of good or bad customer service.)

CHAPTER TWO

HONEY, DO YOU LOVE ME?

HOW YOU COMMUNICATE MEANS EVERYTHING

Has this ever happened to you? You are with your wife or girlfriend, husband or boyfriend, and you can tell something is wrong. So you ask your sweetie pie, very gently, "Are you OK?" What you are actually thinking is, "Is it me? Did I do something wrong?" And really the question beneath it all is, "Honey, do you love me?"

And what does your sweetie pie say? With her legs crossed, her arms folded, her mouth tight, not making eye contact with you, she says, "No, everything's fine." Pop quiz: Is everything fine?

Not on your life, and you know it. She might as well be standing on the couch screaming at you, because you know that's how she feels.

We all know the signs the people we love display when they are not happy. With practice, we can get just as good at reading our customers' thoughts and feelings. We also need to develop enough confidence in our own skills that when we see these "something's not right" signals, we know we can determine what's wrong and fix it.

Here is the story of "Aunt Polly and the Little Boy." Aunt Polly was single and about 60 years old, she dressed in browns and grays, and, her voice was soft, when she spoke at all. Her hair was long and tied tightly back, and her gestures were modest and subdued. When the little boy was 5 years old, Aunt Polly moved to Italy.

When Aunt Polly came back for her first visit two years later, her hair was long and frizzy and, she talked in a sing-song voice, and, she wore a bright print dress with red and yellow flowers. When the little boy saw her he was dumbfounded. His eyes popped wide, his jaw dropped and he could barely say, "hello." Everyone, including Aunt Polly, laughed. Later, his mother said, "Seeing Aunt Polly again really made an impression on you."

"What do you mean?" the boy said.

"Your eyes were wide, your mouth was open and you were staring," his mother replied.

"Oh," the boy said. "I guess I forgot to control my face."

As adults, sometimes we fool ourselves into thinking we can "control our faces" well enough to conceal what we are thinking and how we feel. The truth is, who we are and what we are thinking or feeling comes through. The truth always comes through loud and clear with our bosses, sweetie pies, customers, co-workers, kids, friends, and even strangers.

When we are with customers and we are distracted, disinterested, displeased or simply bored, they can tell within three or four seconds.

How do they know? We tell them.

The findings below are based upon research done at The Harvard School of Linguistics. Before we look at their findings, take this fast quiz to see how people communicate face-to-face.

COMMUNICATION (IN PERSON)

The percentages should add up to 100%.

____ % Words

____ % Tone

____ % Body Language

Answers: See page 56

COMMUNICATION (BY TELEPHONE)

The percentages should add up to 100%.

____ % Words

____ % Tone

____ % Body Language

Answers: See page 57

COMMUNICATION (BY EMAIL OR TEXTING)

The percentages should add up to 100%.

____ % Words

____ % Tone

____ % Body Language

Answers: See page 58

An Honest Assessment

Now let's look at how the following set of skills contributes to your ability to communicate. Give yourself 1, 2 or 3 depending on which description of the **attribute in bold** fits your ability level.

Your ability to **stay focused:**
1. I'm very often unfocused.
2. I focus well, but I could use improvement.
3. I'm usually focused.

Your ability to **be organized:**
1. I'm rather disorganized.
2. I could use coaching on staying organized.
3. I'm mostly organized.

Your ability to **be punctual:**
1. I'm almost always late.
2. I need support being on time.
3. I'm almost never late.

Your ability to **maintain an upbeat attitude:**
1. I whine a lot.
2. My mood depends on the day.
3. I smile most of the time.

Your ability to **project positive energy:**
1. People see me as having negative energy.
2. I'm inconsistent with the energy I project.
3. I'm a positive-energy person.

Your ability to **do your job independently:**
1. I'm a high-maintenance employee.
2. I sometimes feel overwhelmed by my job.
3. I'm a low-maintenance employee.

HONEY, DO YOU LOVE ME?

Add your scores and look at the three columns on the next page.

A score of 6 – 10 puts your communication abilities in the column on the left, along with 30% of customer service workers.

A score of 11 – 15 puts you in the center column, with 40% of customer service workers.

A score of 16 – 18 puts you in the column on the right, with the top 30% of customer service workers.

RATE OF PRODUCTIVITY BY EMPLOYEE CATEGORY		
BOTTOM	MIDDLE	TOP
30%	**40%**	**30%**
↓ 40 - 45% PRODUCTIVITY	70 - 75% PRODUCTIVITY	85% PRODUCTIVITY ↑
unfocused	good, not great	focused
unorganized	need coaching	organized
always late	need support	never late
whine a lot	mood depends on the day	smile a lot
negative energy	inconsistent	positive energy
high maintenance	overwhelmed	low maintenance

This book and my seminars are about helping you to honestly look at how you perform in the workplace and in your personal life. It's the same with these exercises. Here's another one!

On the next page, read the description on the left and rate yourself on the right. "How often do you smile?" Is it 10% of the time? 80%? If it's 10% put a 1, if it's 80% put an 8. So, look to the numbers to the right of these qualities as percentage of the time you perform them.

The purpose of this assessment is simply to show you where to focus your efforts toward improvement. Start with one of the qualities where you gave yourself a low score. Work on that for the next month. Let's say you gave yourself a 3 for saying "Thank You" because most of the time you feel like you are too busy to say "Thank You" with any sincerity. Here is your task: For the next three weeks practice saying "Thank You" to every customer, co-worker, vendor, family member and stranger that you encounter. It will feel odd, strange and insincere at times, but remember you are developing a skill and that's never easy. Experts say "it takes 21 days of repetition to create a habit." After three weeks, "Thank You" should be part of your everyday vocabulary.

Don't stop now...keep on saying "Thank You," and now add the person's name. Do this on a regular basis and it will make a huge difference in your life. In just 12 months, you could perfect 12 different customer service qualities allowing you to better serve your customers and co-workers, too!

Read the description on the left and rate yourself on the right.

Smile	1 2 3 4 5 6 7 8 9 10
Eye Contact	1 2 3 4 5 6 7 8 9 10
Friendly Welcome	1 2 3 4 5 6 7 8 9 10
Use Their Name	1 2 3 4 5 6 7 8 9 10
Exceed Expectations	1 2 3 4 5 6 7 8 9 10
Say "Thank You"	1 2 3 4 5 6 7 8 9 10
Invite Them Back	1 2 3 4 5 6 7 8 9 10
Self Confident	1 2 3 4 5 6 7 8 9 10
Patient	1 2 3 4 5 6 7 8 9 10
A "Salesperson"	1 2 3 4 5 6 7 8 9 10
Punctual	1 2 3 4 5 6 7 8 9 10
Good Listener	1 2 3 4 5 6 7 8 9 10
Product Knowledge	1 2 3 4 5 6 7 8 9 10

Remember that a person's name is to that person the sweetest and most important sound in any language.

— HOW TO WIN FRIENDS AND INFLUENCE PEOPLE
DALE CARNEGIE

HONEY, DO YOU LOVE ME?

BECOMING A MASTER AT DETECTING THE TRUTH

Now let's turn things around. Body language is a two-way street. Customers are good at reading our body language, but we can learn to read theirs too.

You can use your listening and observations skills to tell whether or not your customers are satisfied with the service they are getting. The key is to be determined and perceptive in watching how they behave. We have to fight the tendency to kid ourselves into believing they are satisfied when in fact they might just be, 'controlling their faces.'

Check out the '7-38-55 Rule' (see page 56) when asking customers if they are happy with the service. Put the least emphasis on what they say, more on their tone, and the most on their body language. Pay careful attention to everything they do.

We all need to be like lawyers and detectives when we listen to our customers talk about the service they've received or are receiving. Lawyers, police investigators, journalists and psychologists are legendary for having accurate BS detectors. A big hit on television in 2010 was *Lie to Me*, whose main character was loosely based on scientist Paul Ekman, "the world's leading deception expert." The show's slogan was, "The truth is written all over our faces."

My friend Steve, who owns the Best Western ClockTower in Billings, Montana, urges his front desk staff to pry if a customer looks down after being asked if everything was OK, even if they say "Yes," because he knows some customers will not tell you and he needs to know of any problems so he can rectify them. They often follow up with a question like, "Is there anything we could have done better?" Or something like this: 'In an effort to create 100% satisfaction, how could we have made your stay even better?' With this kind of questioning the customer feels like the staff really cares and will be more likely to share a bad experience if they had one. The point is that we need to become world-class detectives, and work hard at paying attention to what our customers are really saying. This line of questioning comes from the best waiter I ever worked with. His name was Chris and we worked together on Rush Street in Chicago. He taught me this lesson: When you ask everyone at the table if the meal is satisfactory, and if anyone gives less than a 100% positive answer, follow up with more specific questions like, "Is the soup hot enough?" or, "Is your steak cooked the way you like it?"

It makes us a little fearful to ask customers if they have received what they want because, in a way we are asking, "Did I do a good job?" It may help to realize that it is difficult, and sometimes impossible, to deliver exactly what someone wants the very first time. When they made their initial request, as in ordering a meal, they might not have known exactly what they wanted. Consequently, the process of asking questions and listening is essential for exceptional service.

Another reason many people don't do a thorough job of following up is because they are afraid it will lead to more work for them. We've all experienced the waiter who breezes by the table and without stopping, gives everyone the "thumbs up," and says, "Everything's great, right?" That guy clearly has no interest in hearing about the drowned salad, the half-cooked meat or the empty water glass. His words are asking if everything is satisfactory, but tone and body language are saying, "I don't have time for you."

When you ask your customer the question, be sure he or she understands you are ready for whatever answer might be given. You aren't asking simply because, "My manager says this is what I'm supposed to do," or, "Our procedure says we have to 'check in' every 30 minutes." With your tone and body language, as well as with your words, communicate the fact that you understand things might not be perfect right now, but that you are willing to do whatever is necessary to make improvements.

Remember, when you take the time to really be present with your customers, you will know how they feel about the service they are receiving. When you listen to them and observe their tone and body language, they won't be able to "control their faces." Know that when you see these "something's not right" signals, you will be able to determine what's not working and fix it.

Becoming a master at detecting the truth means you will always know where your attention needs to go next. This is a skill you can use in all areas of your life; when asking your kids how school went today, listening to your mom tell you (or try to avoid telling you) about her health, listening to your real estate agent estimating the value of your house, or when you ask your sweetie pie, "Honey, do you love me?"

ACTIVE LISTENING

As you can see, listening is the key to knowing how your customer truly feels. One of the best ways to make sure you understand what he or she is saying, is to paraphrase it. This is sometimes called "*active listening.*" It might sound like this: "Just so I'm sure I understand, did you mean, if you receive your order within two weeks, everything will be fine? But you're concerned that if it doesn't ship until 10 days from now, you won't have it within two weeks?"

Honey, Do You Love Me?

Below are possible phrases you can use when you are not sure you have understood your customer.

(Please circle the ones that best fit your way of thinking)

It sounds like you...

So just to clarify...

Let me just go over this to make sure I have it right...

What I hear you say is...

You mean...

Could it be that...

I wonder if...

I'm not sure if I'm with you, so...

What I believe I hear you saying is...

Correct me if I'm wrong, it sounds like...

Is it possible that...

Does it sound reasonable that...

Perhaps you're feeling...

As I hear it, you...

If you were working with someone you just met, and five minutes later are asked to communicate a simple, two-part thought like...

"If you receive your order within two weeks everything will be fine, but you are concerned that if it doesn't ship until 10 days from now, you won't have it in time."

- How confident would you be that that typical person could understand it and repeat it to you or to a third party?

- How much would you be willing to bet on it?

Having worked inside dozens of companies, I know that communication is almost always cited as one of the most critical problems. When companies ask their employees for ideas on improving operations, communication usually comes up as the #1 response.

There's a simple reason for this: communicating is challenging. Fill in the quick survey below and I'll show you why.

WHAT WE SAY AND WHAT IT MEANS

Directions: *In each space below, indicate what you feel would be the percentage equivalent of the underlined word or phrase.*

EXAMPLE: If something occurred HALF THE TIME, it would occur 50% of the time.

1. If something occurred **OCCASIONALLY,** it would occur_____% of the time.

2. If something occurred **SOMETIMES**, it would occur_____% of the time

3. If something occurred **NOW AND THEN**, it would occur_____% of the time

You might think this survey is about the meanings of words and terms used to describe frequency. It is not. The purpose of this exercise is to look at how widely our ways of describing things vary. It is about how challenging communication can be, and how important it is that we speak and listen with great care and precision.

I have been using this exercise in my seminars for many years and participants frequently write numbers that differ drastically.

For instance, in a recent seminar, answering the first question, a woman named Jennifer wrote down 70%.

Sitting in the very next seat, her co-worker, Dave, wrote, 5%. I asked them to talk about a problem that occurs in their work "occasionally." Then I asked them to talk about different approaches to it. Here's how their conversation went.

Jennifer says, "This is a big problem, Dave. It's something that happens occasionally and we have to deal with it."

But Dave says, "It's not a big deal, it only happens occasionally."

Jennifer says, "Dave, you're apathetic. We need to do something about it." But Dave says, "Calm down, you worry about everything and you stress out the team for no reason."

Now they are banging heads over something they both agree on! It's a problem that happens "occasionally."

For #2, a participant named Carey wrote 1% for "sometimes" and Angel wrote 10%.

These results come from people who work for the same company and know each other well.

Compared to what they face, how challenging is it to communicate with a customer you've never met, who lives in a different state, in a different time zone, and with whom you might have very little in common?

Communicating is not as simple as we think. It's easy to assume people understand what we are saying because the thought we are trying to express is clear to us! But the problem is that we see things differently. That's not a bad thing. Our backgrounds, our upbringing, our cultural roots, our generations, all contribute to the great mix of people we are. We wouldn't want that to change. But our differences are a big part of our communication challenges. Even when we're with people with whom we share cultural, ethnic, religious, and even generational similarities, it can still be challenging to communicate!

Over time, social scientists have learned that human beings break into four basic personalities or temperaments. This is true even for people who come from the same tribe. Different observers have given a variety of names and descriptions to these four personalities. For our purposes, let's call them

- Analysts
- Drivers
- Expressives
- Amiables

Following are some of each group's typical attributes.

ANALYTICALS

Value data, value accuracy and precision, focus on facts over intuition, tend to be cautious, reserved, independent, and aloof.

You might hear them say:

☐ Let's study this for another month, and then maybe we'll decide.

☐ You expect me to understand this without a single chart or graph?

☐ The only team member I need (or want) is my very sharp pencil.

☐ A week's worth of numbers and details? Let's party!

☐ You were off by .oool. That's not what I call, "Accurate."

☐ I'd hug you but I'm happier behind my big, cozy desk.

Their Best	Their Worst
Careful	Inflexible
Thorough	Indecisive
Intelligent	Uncooperative

DRIVERS

Tend to be results-oriented, ambitious, aggressive, purposeful, enterprising, and direct.

You might hear them say:

❑ Thanks for coming to my meeting. Now sit down. I'm in charge.

❑ What's more important than the bottom line? Oxygen. Maybe.

❑ Let's talk business. You've got 5 minutes.

❑ I'm not competitive, but I bet my shoes cost more than yours.

❑ Why are we waiting? Time is money.

❑ I'm sorry your dog was hit by a car. Now, here's my PowerPoint.

Their Best	Their Worst
Leadership	Insensitive
Perseverance	Stubborn
Achievement	Selfish

EXPRESSIVES

Display aversion to details, tend to be sociable, intuitive, enthusiastic, friendly, and forthcoming.

You might hear them say:

- ❏ I haven't read it, but I get the idea.
- ❏ The important thing is the big picture, and the big picture is…
- ❏ Let's grab some lunch so we can talk about this.
- ❏ I know a guy who knows a woman and she knows this other guy.…..
- ❏ I have this gut feeling about.…..
- ❏ Nice to meet you.

Their Best	Their Worst
Enthusiastic	Impulsive
Persuasive	Careless
Inspiring	Uninformed

Amiables

Display aversion to conflict and concern for others' feelings; avoid the spotlight; tend to be empathetic and placid.

You might hear them say:

- ☐ Tell me about yourself and your situation.
- ☐ Maybe I can help you with that problem.
- ☐ This is how we plan to proceed. Is that all right with you?
- ☐ I'd rather not take the lead, but I'll support you.
- ☐ I'm afraid that would make them upset.

Their Best	Their Worst
Helpful	Vague
Peacemakers	Superficial
Flexible	Weak

These four personality categories are generalizations. Every person, though falling basically into one of these four, has attributes of the other three as well.

The lesson is that we have to ask and listen, ask and observe, and, perhaps even ask a third time, in order to accurately understand someone else's experience.

If you are working with four people, one from each of

the four types, and each one responds to your query about the service they've received with the answer, "Fine," they might be telling you four very different things.

The "Analytical" might be saying, "I'm not sure, I haven't decided yet." The "Driver" might be saying, "The service has been so-so, but I don't think it's worth my time to talk to you about how it could be better." The "Expressive" might be saying, "I think I understand what you are asking, but let's just move on." And the "Amiable" might be saying, " I really enjoyed that one thing you did, but I was really disappointed in the other six elements; however, I don't want to upset you."

We also need to take into account our own personalities. Are you an "Expressive?" If so, be aware that when interacting with an "Analytical," you're likely to feel impatient; he or she is naturally much slower to arrive at a conclusion. If you are an "Amiable," know that your "Driver" co-worker, with their intense eye contact standing so close and speaking so loudly isn't doing so because he or she is inappropriate; rather, it's their nature. The orientation of their personality is to behave this way.

the four types, and each one responds to your query about the service they've received with the answer, "Fine," they might be telling you four very different things.

The "Analytical" might be saying, "I'm not sure, I haven't decided yet." The "Driver" might be saying, "The service has been so-so, but I don't think it's worth my time to talk to you about how it could be better." The "Expressive" might be saying, "I think I understand what you are asking, but let's just move on." And the "Amiable" might be saying, " I really enjoyed that one thing you did, but I was really disappointed in the other six elements; however, I don't want to upset you."

We also need to take into account our own personalities. Are you an "Expressive?" If so, be aware that when interacting with an "Analytical," you're likely to feel impatient; he or she is naturally much slower to arrive at a conclusion. If you are an "Amiable," know that your "Driver" co-worker, with their intense eye contact standing so close and speaking so loudly isn't doing so because he or she is inappropriate; rather, it's their nature. The orientation of their personality is to behave this way.

DRIVERS

Tend to be results-oriented, ambitious, aggressive, purposeful, enterprising, and direct.

You might hear them say:

☐ Thanks for coming to my meeting. Now sit down. I'm in charge.

☐ What's more important than the bottom line? Oxygen. Maybe.

☐ Let's talk business. You've got 5 minutes.

☐ I'm not competitive, but I bet my shoes cost more than yours.

☐ Why are we waiting? Time is money.

☐ I'm sorry your dog was hit by a car. Now, here's my PowerPoint.

Their Best	Their Worst
Leadership	Insensitive
Perseverance	Stubborn
Achievement	Selfish

EXPRESSIVES

Display aversion to details, tend to be sociable, intuitive, enthusiastic, friendly, and forthcoming.

You might hear them say:

- ❏ I haven't read it, but I get the idea.
- ❏ The important thing is the big picture, and the big picture is…
- ❏ Let's grab some lunch so we can talk about this.
- ❏ I know a guy who knows a woman and she knows this other guy…..
- ❏ I have this gut feeling about…..
- ❏ Nice to meet you.

Their Best	Their Worst
Enthusiastic	Impulsive
Persuasive	Careless
Inspiring	Uninformed

AMIABLES

Display aversion to conflict and concern for others' feelings; avoid the spotlight; tend to be empathetic and placid.

You might hear them say:

- ❏ Tell me about yourself and your situation.
- ❏ Maybe I can help you with that problem.
- ❏ This is how we plan to proceed. Is that all right with you?
- ❏ I'd rather not take the lead, but I'll support you.
- ❏ I'm afraid that would make them upset.

Their Best	Their Worst
Helpful	Vague
Peacemakers	Superficial
Flexible	Weak

These four personality categories are generalizations. Every person, though falling basically into one of these four, has attributes of the other three as well.

The lesson is that we have to ask and listen, ask and observe, and, perhaps even ask a third time, in order to accurately understand someone else's experience.

If you are working with four people, one from each of

Honey, Do You Love Me?

A Commitment to Yourself

Olympic athletes know they will never become so good at their sport that they can stop training. In the same way, I know I have to work on my communication skills every day. It's impossible for us to ever get too good at communicating.

Here are eight communication skills you can work on every day:

Eight Action Steps To Improving Your Customer Service Through Effective Communication Skills

1. **Have a warm welcome.**
   Extend your hand, look the person in the eye, and smile. Beware of cultural differences.

2. **Eye contact.**
   Looking into someone's eyes makes him feel like they matter. Connecting through eye contact creates trust. Not looking someone in the eye creates suspicion.

3. **Be aware of your volume.**
   Make sure you're not too loud or too soft.

4. **Speak clearly and annunciate, especially when answering the phone.**
   An inability to understand quickly becomes a reason to stop listening. Make sure you don't talk too fast or too slow.

5. **Be aware of your body language.**
   55% of your face-to-face communication is body language (see page 56).

6. **Listen from the other person's point of view.**
   Put yourself in their shoes.

7. **Ask great questions.**
   Ask questions that invite people to share all their concerns so you can serve them better.

8. **Say it with enthusiasm.**
   Add energy to what you're saying; it will be better received.

Every worthwhile endeavor begins with a commitment and a plan.

You can do both by creating a plan and committing to it. To get started, write your answers in the following five sections:

Personal Performance-Plan of Action

1. I will improve my communications with my customers by:

   _____

   _____

   _____

   _____

   _____

   _____

   _____

2. I will improve my communications with my co-workers by:

   _____

   _____

   _____

   _____

   _____

   _____

   _____

PLAN OF ACTION (CONTINUED)

3. I will improve my communications with other
    departments by:

    _____

    _____

    _____

    _____

    _____

    _____

    _____

4. I will improve my communications with my
    manager by:

    _____

    _____

    _____

    _____

    _____

    _____

    _____

PLAN OF ACTION (CONTINUED)

5. I will improve my communications with my spouse, children, siblings, partner, best friend, etc. by:

_____

_____

_____

_____

_____

_____

_____

_____

_____

_____

_____

_____

_____

_____

_____

_____

_____

Answers: Communication (In Person)

Here is what the Harvard Linguistics School study found:
7% Words
38% Tone
55% Body Language

Most people predict their words will carry much more weight than 7%.

This is the "7-38-55 rule." We are all capable of detecting when a customer is satisfied or not by this rule. You must pay close attention after asking if everything was OK and they say 'Yes' in an unenthusiastic way. Are they just saying that to appease you? Further investigation should go into full swing by asking questions. When we ask, we've got to make sure our tone of voice is emphatic and want to hear their feedback because it might not be so great.

When we are serving our customers or clients these figures are just as important because a customer will be able to tell if we really want to serve them in a few seconds.

ANSWERS TO COMMIUNICATION QUIZES ON PAGE 31

How about the phone? Many of you reading this book are sales reps or customer service reps who are on the phone all day long.

Answers: Communication (By Telephone)

14% Words
86% Tone
0% Body Language

Many, many, many people disagree with the 0% for Body Language. I did too at first, but the reason it's zero is because they can't see you. Does slouching playing an important part when you are on the phone? Yep! Does 'not smiling' play an important part when you answer the phone? Yep! Does smiling play an important part when you answer the phone? Yep! Body language is felt through your tone, so that's why tone is the remaining 86%. When the phone rings at your business you want to do a little happy dance and answer it with enthusiasm (note: the happy dance should take about a second). Also, don't forget the first hour of your day sets the tone for the rest of the day and the first two-three seconds of your phone conversation or face-to-face sets the tone for that interaction. Trust is determined in that short time.

How about e-mailing and texting? Sometimes it seems like this is the only way we communicate, so these percentages could be the most important.

Answers: Communication (By Email or Text)

100% Words
0% Tone
0% Body Language

Again I get pushback because people say tone comes through e-mail and I totally agree, yet remember all they have when they get your e-mail or text is words on a screen, so make sure you are clear with your message. I recommend using please and thank you in all e-mails or texts, business or personal. Texting is a little more informal, but I still recommend using "please" and "thank you" in texting because it's just as important as it is in an e-mail.

Chapter Three

Do It For Whom?

Taking Care of Customer #1

There has always been a giant unanswered question in customer service that no one wants to touch. "Where does it all come from?" The big, authentic, enthusiastic smile you offer everyone, the kind, measured response you give, even to someone who is being unkind, argumentative, or is treating you like you're an idiot, "Where does it all come from?"

Is it supposed to be a natural part of your skill set? Were you born with an endless supply of sweetness, kindness, and patience?

Does it come with the job? After you cash your first paycheck do you suddenly possess a super-human ability to understand what people want, even when they aren't clear on what they want themselves?

I remember when I was waiting tables, and a woman came into the restaurant with a party of eight. I presented the specials and answered a few questions about the menu. I took the lunch orders of all seven other diners while she perused the menu. Finally, all eyes turned her way, but she continued deliberating... carefully, slowly, as if the fate of the world rested on her choice. Everyone at the big table was quiet and the silence spilled out into the rest of the room. The other wait staff stopped and turned; bus boys put down their trays, conversations stopped, and the maitre' d' looked from across the room. When she asked me a question about the pasta it seemed like she might be getting close. I looked around at my other tables thinking of all the things I needed to be doing. When she looked up at me with a blank stare I nearly threw my pen at her. Finally, she looked at one of her dining companions and said, "Do I like Roquefort dressing?"

I stood there, speechless, a fake smile frozen on my face. Everyone who was there will remember for the rest of their lives the desperation they felt living through that moment with the Roquefort Lady.

The Roquefort Lady may be the world's nicest person. She might hold the record at her church for most volunteer hours served, or be the person in the neighborhood who always finds the lost puppy and brings it back to its owners, but in this moment, it was completely understandable that I and a dozen other people in the restaurant wanted to leap across the table and strangle her.

What did I do? I smiled. I offered to give her a moment to finish making her selection. I asked if anyone at the table wanted another drink. I told myself to let it go and not walk into the kitchen complaining a blue streak about the crazy lady at table 5. In other words, I did the things we all know to do when faced with a challenging customer.

But the bigger question no one thinks to ask—or answer — is, where was I supposed to find the endless stream of wonderfulness allowing me to deal with the Roquefort Lady? This perfect blend of kindness, patience and understanding?

The answer is, by treating yourself as well as you treat your customers, taking care of yourself first, and making yourself Customer #1.

Think of the announcement made on every airline flight—"Put your own mask on first before helping those around you." You are not expected to go without oxygen so that you can make sure others can breathe easy. In fact, the opposite is true. By taking care of yourself first, only then are you able to help others.

We shouldn't kid ourselves, we really do help people. Customer service has been a major part of every job I've ever had. In that regard, I've worked in customer service my entire career. I know firsthand we have the power to take an ordinary moment and make it extraordinary. I know that with something as simple as a smile, or with the unexpectedly helpful remark, we can take a hum-drum event and make it special. I have realized that giving people what they need in a way that it makes them feel good is powerful for them and rewarding for us. And it's fun and exhilarating, too!

I regularly get heartfelt emails and messages from people telling me I've made a difference in their lives. I've been a seminar leader and speaker for more than 20 years, but each time it's still a surprise. Being thanked by someone I don't know well and worked with only briefly is the last thing I expected when I began this work, but it's incredibly gratifying.

I remember the first time I got a handwritten letter from a man who said I had changed his life. I couldn't believe something I had done had been part of creating such a profound effect. I don't take full credit for it because I know I can't change anyone's life. Only you can change your life. You are the one who does the work to advance (as I am in mine). But it still puts a charge in me, and I take it as a great honor when I hear I brought something that helped someone create profound, positive change.

Of course, from a purely business standpoint, I follow up with people to find out how my work has been received. From all of the feedback over 20 years, the extraordinary as well as the routine, I've learned two things:

First, we can't control how people will respond to what we do. Second, we have an effect on everyone we encounter: what we do flows outward like ripples in a pond, whether we see them moving or not.

Do It For Whom?

There is also a point in us all, where we are aware of what kind of a job we do, and I know it matters. If you aren't giving it everything you can, you won't feel great.

How you do what you do affects everyone you come in contact with, because how you do what you do at your job especially matters to you. There's that place inside that says, if you aren't giving it everything you can, you won't feel great; so do it great! Sometimes the work can be draining, and you can feel worn out, wrung out and exhausted or you leave your job at the end of the day feeling satisfied, stimulated and fulfilled. That's why it's important to:

Make Yourself Customer #1 Every Day!

How do you do that? Let's begin with this question:

When Does Customer Service Start?

Many people think customer service begins with the first customer of the day, or when their shift starts. Others suggest it begins while driving to work or walking into work from the parking lot.

How about this? Exceptional Customer Service begins as soon as your eyes open in the morning, the instant your feet hit the floor. Why? Because that's when you first encounter Customer #1...YOU!

Give Yourself This Amazing Gift and Make Every Day a Great Day!

Learn the following five simple steps to make sure that you treat yourself as Customer #1. It will be one of the best things you'll do in your entire life. Even greater is the fact that you can use these tools ... every day.

Five things you can do every day to make sure you take care of Customer #1.

1. **CHOOSE TO HAVE A GREAT DAY.** It couldn't be simpler than that. Just make the decision that today is going to be a great day. Visualize wonderful things that will happen to you throughout the course of the day. Decide you are going to enjoy your day, no matter what happens.

2. **START WITH YOURSELF.** Take responsibility for your life—it's too precious to leave in someone else's hands. Besides, it's your life. The thrill and enjoyment of making your life the way you want it to be belongs to you.

   I used to see a woman buying coffee and a lottery ticket every morning. She was a grim-faced woman, one of those people who seem to be slogging down their path in life with heavy steps, as if the road is always muddy. I attempted to greet her a few times, but her response was always tepid, so I finally gave up.

Then one day I saw her at the cash register buying her coffee but no lottery ticket and I couldn't help myself. "What about your ticket?" I said. "Today could be the day."

"I'm not playing the lottery any more," she said to me, and she was smiling, actually beaming. I had never seen her like this. I couldn't believe it. She was a completely different person.

"Why not?" I said.

"Because I don't want to win. I started my own business; I want to make my fortune myself," she said.

And that was it. She took her coffee and she was gone, off to her new business, and I never saw her again. But I completely understood. She had taken control of her life. She wasn't leaving happiness, success, her experience of her own precious life, up to fate or the people she worked with or anybody else. She realized that her happiness and her success were up to her.

3. **APPRECIATE YOUR LIFE.** Each of us is a miracle of nature. To experience human life is the greatest gift on earth.

And there is so much more than that. Our lives are filled with more good things than we can count. It's no wonder we lose track and take things like clean sheets, oxygen, and pure drinking water for granted.

How many good things can you think of (that you appreciate) in the time it takes you to brush your teeth?

4. **AFFIRM YOUR DAY.** This is one of the most powerful tools that I have ever known.

Your thoughts are endlessly powerful, and they work behind the scenes to create your reality. The first step in creating the world we want is to put those thoughts into words.

Think of the great leaders and reformers and you'll see that most of their leadership flowed from their words. Whether it's Franklin Delano Roosevelt saying, "We have nothing to fear but fear itself," President John F. Kennedy saying, "Ask not what your country can do for you, ask rather what you can do for your country," or Martin Luther King, Jr. saying, "I have a dream," in every case, action was preceded by words. Those words were driven by thoughts and, in every case, those thoughts were carefully chosen. Roosevelt chose courage in a time when many were locked in fear; Kennedy chose contribution and sacrifice in a time when many people were asleep in selfishness; and King chose hope over despair.

The word, "declare" reminds us we have the power to create something out of nothing, using only our words. The historian, John McCullough, tells us that on July 4, 1776, the Founding Fathers sat in stunned silence after they voted for the Declaration of Independence. They looked around the room at one another while the magnitude of what they did sank in. They had just declared a new country into being. Moments ago, there was no United States of America. Now there was.

What do you want to declare into being? You can do it with your life, with your day. You can do it by declaring that you are Customer #1. You can do it today.

reasonableness. I probably *can't* have abs like a movie actor, right? I'm probably *not* cut out to be a CEO. It *really is* hard to be upbeat in the dead of winter when the days are short and there's hardly any sunlight. That's a scientific fact, right? Those are all reasonable statements, aren't they?

An effective liar always starts with a kernel of truth and then twists it into a story that works to his or her advantage. That's how funk operates. It's true that I don't have abs like a movie actor. It might also be true that I don't have access to a top personal trainer, like the actor, or that I'm not 25 years old like the actor.

But it's not true that you can't look and feel great, and it's possible that nothing is preventing you from having a healthy body, a strong core and fit abdominal muscles. You can exercise, swim, ride a bike, do yoga, and adopt a host of diet and health habits that are great for you physically and mentally.

Another characteristic of funk; it grows. Like an acorn becomes an oak tree, funk can grow from a tiny sticky note of a complaint into a giant **"Life Stinks!"** billboard. It can happen quickly too.

A man I'll call Jason worked in a particular department at a large company and hoped to move into management. After he had made one request and was rejected, he thought that his company didn't promote

Chapter Four

Leave Your Funk at the Door

Taking charge of your 'Funk'

What is funk?

Funk is your garbage, your baggage. It's your argument for what's wrong with the world, what's wrong with you, why life isn't fair, why things aren't working out, and why they are not going to work out. It doesn't do you any good. It doesn't help you accomplish anything. It doesn't make life easier or better in any way. It is unbecoming and does not serve you.

Your funk doesn't do anything good for anyone else either. Your funk affirms for the people around you that they live in a world of funk. Your funk feeds their funk and vice-versa.

It is true that funk serves no purpose, but it's worse than that: funk holds us back. Going through life focusing on our funk is like running a race carrying a garbage can.

Most of us spend a good amount of energy staying focused on what we want to accomplish and moving in that direction. Funk points us in the opposite direction and slows us down on our trip.

Still, we all have funk.

Below is what funk sounds like. See if you recognize

people from his department into management. The first couple times that he groused about it to his friends in his department, he used the words, "*I don't think they promote people from our department.*" But that statement soon became, "They don't promote from our department," and then, "They never promote from our department." It was repeated so often that people started to believe it. For a time, it appeared to be true, because there weren't any former members of Jason's department recently promoted to management. Meanwhile, Jason never made a second attempt at advancing. Why should he try? The company never promoted from his department.

Then senior management promoted a woman named Tina from Jason's department. Tina had been taking appropriate courses, made several inquiries and requests, and had not participated in the conversations about the company not promoting from her department. Jason was left feeling quite embarrassed.

What he learned about funk, however, is that it can grow from a thought into an opinion, from an opinion into a perceived fact, and finally, from a perceived fact into a story that takes over the situation.

If you examine your funk, if you compare it side by side with the truth, funk won't hold up. Funk is fiction. It falls apart when attacked with the simple truth that, "Where there's a will, there's a way."

Be careful not to fall in love with your funk. Funk is capable of getting us to fight for it. Sometimes we treat it so well—we nurture it, embellish it, treat it like a cherished member of the family. Then whatever story our funk is inspiring us to tell becomes more elaborate, more detailed, more real, and appears more and more to be the truth.

I had a teacher who showed me how we love to fight for our opinions and for our stories even when we know they aren't helping. One time, he asked my friend Alice to organize an event for the evening of March 17th. Alice pointed out that March 17th is St. Patrick's Day and, in Chicago, that's an evening most people spend at parties and taverns. "We only need 20 people to attend in order to have a successful event," our teacher said. "In a city of 3 million, isn't that possible, even though it's St. Patrick's Day?" he asked.

"No," Alice told him, "not really. Chicago is a very Irish city." But our teacher decided not to change the date, so Alice started working on the event. It was very hard for her because she grew up in Chicago and was aware of the St. Patrick's Day traditions—parades, dinners, parties. It seemed quite reasonable that no one would pass on all of that to do something different. Her funk was screaming at her, "This will never work!"

Nevertheless she talked to people, sent out notices, and made some calls. When no one responded she went back to our teacher and presented the proof that she had been right. No one was coming. Everyone was celebrating St. Patrick's Day.

Our teacher thanked Alice for giving it her best effort, then turned the event over to Maureen. Maureen is Irish and knew better than anyone how challenging the task was.

"What are you going to do?" I asked her.

"I'm going to invite people," she said.

"Yea, but aren't you worried that..." I had bought into the funk. I thought it was hopeless.

Maureen cut me off. "Don't say it," she said. "If I get stuck in that, it will never work."

Maureen got 40 people to come to the event. They all wore green. It was a huge success.

At the event, Alice was sulking. Some of the people she originally invited showed up, including friends, and members of her family, so she shared in the credit. But even as it was all happening right before her eyes, she couldn't let go of her funk. It was so persuasive, she believed in funk more than reality.

Sometimes we fight for our funk just because it's ours.

Beware of enrolling people in your funk. Stay away from people who agree with you when you unpack your funk, when you tell your sad tale of woe.

Here are some more examples of funk:

Life Isn't Fair Funk
- I never win anything.
- They discriminate against my (race, gender, age, nationality, regional origin, fashion sense...almost anything will do here).

It Wasn't My Fault Funk
- They just don't like me.
- I did my best, but it wasn't good enough.
- They didn't explain what was required.
- They cheated.

I'm Stuck Funk
- I'm in debt and there's no way out.
- I can't do _____ because of my kids/my parents/my dog.

I Want It But I Can't Have It Funk
- It costs too much.
- My spouse won't agree.
- "They" won't let me.

LEAVE YOUR FUNK AT THE DOOR

WHAT SHOULD WE DO ABOUT OUR FUNK?

Ironically, it's easy to get rid of your funk. **Just let it go!** That's all there is to it.

Your keys, purse, wallet, credit cards, these are all things you shouldn't leave lying around. These are things you should be careful with.

But not your funk. No one is interested in taking your funk. When you go to work in the morning, you can leave your funk at the door. It won't harm anyone, it won't take up any space, no one is going to take it. Don't worry about your funk. At the end of the day, it will be there, right where you left it.

When you leave your funk at the door, you are free to walk into work singing a different song: "The sun is shining in my life! I am happy and appreciative that I am here and I'm alive! I'm having a great day!"

Who benefits when you leave your funk at the door? Your customers? You bet. Will your boss and your co-workers be better off? Yes, they will. Your family? Yep! But don't do it for them. The person who will get the most out of you leaving your funk at the door, is YOU! Do it for you!

Don't take my word for it. Try it. When you go into work or wherever your day takes you, as you pass through the doorway, think about your funk and consciously leave it outside. See what happens! Notice if you are happier, lighter, more focused and/or optimistic. See if you don't have more success, even if only a little, and be open to huge changes. See if things become much better.

If you are willing to leave your funk at the door, then you are ready for the advanced game. Here it is:

If you let go of your funk, what takes its place? It's smart to take that space and fill it with something else, because funk has a sneaky way of creeping back in.

The advanced game of Leave Your Funk at the Door® is replacing funk with something better. Positive thoughts, encouragement, affirmations, prayer, and inspirational stories are all much better and healthier alternatives to funk. They create a healthier diet for your heart and your mind.

Remember, leave your funk at the door. It will be there when you get back.

Or maybe going through your day without it, you'll realize you never needed it in the first place.

CHAPTER FIVE

IS THE CUSTOMER ALWAYS RIGHT?

Have you ever wondered who the person is who said, "The customer is always right?" Maybe you've pondered that question while cursing under your breath at someone who's come up with an objection to your every attempt to serve them well?

Customers are not always princes and princesses. Sometimes they're miserable. I know because I've been that miserable customer. I've been the guy in the foul mood who's having a bad day and doesn't care who knows about it or suffers because of it. Those occasions have been rare, but in those moments I was not pleasant to deal with. And I certainly made it difficult for anyone to treat me like I was a deserving customer.

Three great businessmen are responsible for originating the expression, "The customer is always right." In the late 1800's, Marshall Field and his partner George Selfridge opened Marshall Field's department store in Chicago. Field and Selfridge worked together until 1901 and in 1906, Selfridge opened the department store in London that bears his name. Around that time, both stores were using the slogan, "The customer is always right." (Field's became part of the Macy's chain in 2006; Selfridge's is still going strong.)

Who was the third genius responsible for the phrase? That would be Cesar Ritz, the French entrepreneur who was well known by 1908 for his philosophy,

"The customer is never wrong." Mr. Ritz, of course, is legendary for creating some of the world's most luxurious hotels whose trademark is outstanding customer service.

The phrase, "The customer is always right," was never meant to be taken literally. It describes an attitude people who are proactive about customer service strive to live up to. It expresses the idea that we treat the customer well no matter how he or she treats us.

I once owned a pizza restaurant in Livingston, Montana (23 miles east of Bozeman) and one night a woman came in to pick up a pizza. The woman, who I would later name "Mrs. 10 Pieces" was beautiful. Her body looked sculpted. She was impeccably dressed, her makeup was perfect, and she had a rigid, "Don't bother me," look about her. She asked that her pizza be cut into 10 pieces, six on one side and four on the other, which was not the way we usually cut our pizzas.

My employee did her best to cut the pizza the way Mrs. 10 Pieces requested, but it wasn't quite what she wanted, and Mrs. 10 Pieces became verbally abusive. She was mean and nasty, and some of the things she said were personal. They weren't comments designed to help the young woman give her what she wanted; they were meant to be cutting and hurtful. Finally, the young woman started to cry, but even then Mrs. 10 Pieces didn't back down.

Another employee called me at home and asked me what they should do. I said, "Refund Mrs. 10 Pieces, and apologize." They gladly gave her the pizza and her money.

Later, I told my employee, a young woman, she had done her best and shouldn't worry about a thing. As the owner of the business, I'm willing for customers to occasionally take out on me whatever negative stuff is going on in their lives. But I'm not willing for people to belittle my employees. I felt toward them as I do about my wife and kids; I loved them.

Two weeks later, as if nothing had ever happened, Mrs. 10 Pieces came in again and asked for her pizza to be cut into 10 pieces. The young woman asked her to please wait a moment, left the front counter and came to the kitchen where I was working. "She's here," my employee said, and I immediately knew by her tone and the look in her eye who she was talking about.

I cut Mrs. 10 Pieces' pizza exactly the way she wanted —first down the middle and then cutting one half into six pieces and the other into four.

When I gave her the pizza I was careful to be cordial and friendly, but at the same time I was very direct. I told Mrs. 10 Pieces she was welcome in my store, but I didn't want her ever to mistreat one of my employees again.

It was as if steel doors came sliding down all around her. She grew even colder than she had been. Her body went completely stiff. All she said was, "I get things my way," and she took her 10 perfect pieces of pizza and left. I never saw her again.

What I learned from Mrs. 10 Pieces is that even with a great effort, we can't reach every customer every time. What pleases me about the story, as I look back on it from a distance of many years, is not that I learned how to cut a pizza into 10 pieces, it's that I stood up for my employees and was actually glad I'd never see Mrs. 10 Pieces again. And, what makes me happy is that the young woman who was working with me survived being mistreated by an incredibly rude and uncaring customer. When we encounter someone who, whether he or she realizes it or not, is trying to undermine us, we need to stay confident; [otherwise it will be difficult to take care of the next customer].

The conventional wisdom about dealing with upset customers says, "Times are tough, business is hard to come by, and we can't afford to lose a single sale." I understand this point of view. A Harris poll measuring the percent of customers who say they will never return to a business after a negative customer-service experience recently jumped from 68 percent to 80 percent.

The stakes are high. Doing less than our best can mean losing a lot.

But I'd rather focus on the positive. **Every time we sense a customer is having a bad experience, it's a great opportunity.** Working with the angry customer can be the best moment of your day. If you have ever taken a customer who was not merely dissatisfied, but was fire-breathing angry with you or your performance or your business, and turned that person around, you know what a thrill it is. People who love customer service hope to be called to the scene when a customer has become irate because they know the chances are ripe for a big win.

Bill Gates has been quoted as saying, *"Angry customers are the greatest source of learning."* If only one customer in 25 tells you he is upset, he is the one to listen to, Gates says. He is the one who has found something that will help you improve how you go about your business.

One day, when I was waiting tables, a customer told my buddy Chris, also a waiter, that there was garlic in his pea soup. Chris had served hundreds of bowls of pea soup at the restaurant; he knew what was in it and there wasn't any garlic. He immediately told the customer all this and, of course, the customer insisted there was garlic in his soup.

As I was listening to this conversation, I remembered that the day before someone said to Chris, "You argue a lot. If you love arguing so much, why don't you go to law school?"

Suddenly, I got it. Right there, at the next table, listening to my buddy Chris argue with a customer who tasted garlic in his soup, I felt like I was exploding with laughter. What was the point? What a dumb thing to argue about. Maybe the man was right. Maybe there was garlic in the soup today. Maybe the chef had changed the recipe. Maybe some garlic fell into the soup pot, or a small piece found its way into the customer's bowl. Maybe the aroma from the shrimp scampi at the table behind him was so strong he was tasting garlic and thought it came from the soup. What was the difference? Arguing about it was ridiculous!

I realized the customer wasn't even complaining; he was just stating what he thought was a curious fact. He just wanted to be heard and sometimes that is all customers want. Being heard means they matter. If they feel like you care about them, they're more likely to return. If they don't think you care, which means what they have to say doesn't matter, they most likely won't return. It's just that simple.

When angry customers believe you care about them, they very well could become allies and tell their friends, family and associates about you and your business. They can also be our greatest source of learning. Below are five behaviors to avoid and nine tips for dealing with an upset customer.

Five Things You Should Not Do When You are With an Angry Customer

1. Cross your arms

2. Tell them to calm down

3. Argue and get defensive

4. Put them on hold without asking

5. Multi-Task (in person or on the phone)

NINE STRATEGIES FOR DEALING WITH AN UPSET CUSTOMER

1. *Listen and take notes*
   This lets them know you value what they are saying. You might also have to relay what their concern is to a supervisor and this will help you prepare. Repeating to them what they have told you will reinforce for them that they have been heard and they may even begin to calm down.

2. *Let them vent; don't interrupt*
   Show them you value what they are saying. Upset customers don't like to be interrupted. Do you?

3. *Ask questions to encourage venting*
   Asking questions and listening will help discover the full extent of the problem and help customers realize you care by your questions.

4. *Don't take anything personally*
   Even if they attempt to make you feel the issue is personal, it isn't.

5. *Be cool, stay calm*
   Staying calm is much easier when you remember it's not personal. One crazy person in the room or on the phone is enough.

6. *Show concern and apologize if necessary*
   It's absolutely appropriate to feel compassionate and be concerned about someone who is upset. The meaning of the word, "apology," does not necessarily mean accepting blame. Rather, it means "a heartfelt expression of concern and a full explanation of one's involvement and a willingness to take responsibility for creating a solution."

7. *Ask, "How would you like to see this resolved?"*
   Asking this question points the conversation toward a resolution and helps a person feel heard. (I'm guessing 60% might say they want a full refund which means 40% will just want to be heard.)

8. *Offer two options*
   You know what you can and can't give away, so offer them two options that you think will best solve the problem when the customer wants a "full refund." This will help them feel involved in creating a solution. Once you've listened to them explain their problem and you've offered options, work with the choice and follow through to a final solution.

9. *Follow through*
   Making sure your customer's problem is resolved is imperative in turning the customer into a loyal customer.

Studies show up to 97% of angry customers become loyal customers if their problem is solved to their satisfaction.

My mother taught me a lesson about compassion that has helped me relate to customers. When I was in the sixth grade, I was on my way to school one morning when one of the nuns came out of the convent and was walking toward the church. I grew up in a Catholic family, my sister was a nun, and there were nuns at our house all the time, so I knew it was important to show them respect.

I said, "Good Morning, Sister," and she looked through me like I wasn't there. There was no smile, no gesture, no words of greeting, not even a nod. When she did that, I thought, "You bad person."

After school I went home and said to my mother, "You won't believe what happened on my way to school this morning," and told her about the sister who looked right through me. I was really upset, but I felt I had behaved properly and I expected my mother to take my side.

All my mother said, was, "Oh," and she looked at me for what seemed like a very long time. Finally she said, "How do you know she didn't just find out her father had died?"

"What?" I said.

"How do you know she didn't just find out she has cancer?"

"I don't know," I said.

"That's right," my mother said. "You don't know. But you stand there in judgment."

My little sixth grade eyes opened that day.

Once, I was doing a customer service seminar on handling irate customers at a call center for Baxter International in Deerfield, IL. A woman raised her hand and said she understood what I was talking about because something just like it had happened to her once.

A man called and started yelling at her. He was screaming and swearing at the woman, and it seemed like he would never stop. "I am sorry, sir," she said, "I am giving you to my supervisor." She then listened while her supervisor, handled the call.

"How can I help you?" her supervisor said. The man again launched into his tirade. The supervisor listened the whole time. She took notes. Every so often she said, "uh-huh," but that was all she said. She was with the man the whole time he was screaming. She didn't contradict anything he said, she didn't defend.

After about 3-4 minutes of ranting he stopped, let out a huge sigh, and began to cry. Through his tears he said his wife of 46 years was dying of cancer and what he wanted was a hospital bed sent to his house so his wife could die at home. The supervisor said, "No problem sir, we'll take care of that for you right away."

My mother was right. We don't know what others are going through so it's up to us to handle their problem if we can. My experience says 90% of people can be satisfied after being upset, 10% are miserable and no matter what, you cannot please them. They are not just having a terrible day; they might be having a terrible life.

Earlier, I talked about how highly dissatisfied customers become highly satisfied customers if whatever they have perceived as wrong is made right. Another word for "highly satisfied" is "loyal," and that's the ultimate goal in customer service. Loyalty is more than turning individuals into customers who are satisfied with today's transaction. Loyalty is more than turning them into customers who are certain to come back again soon. The home run in customer service is turning customers into people who will sing your praises wherever they go.

Know that dealing with angry customers puts you on the edge of learning great things. It gives you the opportunity to live in the moment because you can't hear what an angry customer is saying and you can't think of an appropriate response unless you are fully present and aware. The only way to succeed with an angry customer is to be at your best, and in the end, isn't that how you want to spend your day—being your best?

CHAPTER SIX

BUT WHAT ABOUT MONDAYS?

CREATING EXCEPTIONAL MOMENTS OF TRUTH

I'm hoping that by now you realize two things about yourself and your efforts to provide Exeptional Customer Service.

- Providing ECS is something you can do. You don't have to be a genius, you don't need a Harvard education, and you don't even need a wealth of experience. You just have to be present with your customer and do your best.

- When you provide ECS the #1 winner is you. Yes, the customer benefits, and your employer and co-workers do, too. In fact, everyone around you benefits. But the person who gets the most out of your doing a great job is..........YOU!

Achieving a level of confidence so that you can provide ECS is a wonderful thing. It feels great to know that you can create satisfied customers, gives you a strength and belief in yourself, and it makes going to work fun.

But how do you make the jump from creating satisfied customers to creating *loyal* customers? How do you go from creating customers who are pleased they spent time and money on your product or service, to creating customers who are so pleased they are certain to come back again and again, and are so excited they can't wait to share their experience with others? How do you create customers who are texting their friends as they walk out of the store, or e-mailing their family the first chance they get?

The secret to getting your customers across the bridge from satisfied to loyal, and from pleased to excited, is consistency.

Remember my story of buying taco seasoning in the grocery store? It took three people treating me with a level of kindness and concern that struck me as way out of the ordinary to ease my worries that I wouldn't find what I needed, that I was late, and that I was going back to my car in the pouring rain without a coat or an umbrella.

That's one form of delivering exceptional customer service where multiple employees each provide ECS which finally breaks through to the customer. It has to be an unbroken chain. For me to have that experience, each employee had to be on his or her game. None of them had any way of knowing that I was a customer who was ready to go over the bridge from satisfied to loyal. They had to be working out of a commitment to provide ECS as a normal part of doing their jobs.

Like any other form of teamwork, it depends on the individual members turning in great performances consistently...every time.

When I make this point in workshops, someone usually asks, "But what about when _____?" You can fill in the blank. You know all the usual gripes and excuses. We've all heard them, and each of us has favorites—these are the moments when we feel it ought to be OK for us not to do a great job. What about at the end of the day when I'm exhausted? What about when I'm in a bad mood? What about when the traffic is horrendous, and it takes me an extra half hour to get to work?

One of the first times I spoke about this in front of a group, the smartest-looking woman in the room stood up to ask a question. She was dressed very neatly and she was wearing dark, professional-looking glasses. She had terrific posture and she spoke beautifully about how she committed every day to give her best performance at work, no matter what. She looked like the girl who got straight A's in school. I couldn't imagine what she was going to ask because she seemed to have it so together.

When she asked her question, "What about Mondays?" not only did I not have an answer for her, I didn't have any idea what she was asking?

Mondays are particularly rough for her, she explained. She treasures her weekends, and she's sorry to see them end. She prefers waking up later in the morning on weekends than she has to on workdays. Her morning commute is often toughest on Monday. The people she works with seem to be in a worse mood on Monday, and she certainly isn't at her cheeriest either. So what about Mondays?

To begin with, Mondays account for 20% of the workweek. That's a hefty chunk. Except for holidays like Memorial Day and Labor Day, which fall on Mondays, Monday is a key part of every workweek. I imagine after a holiday weekend, the problems people associate with Monday just roll over to Tuesday.

If we allow ourselves to fall into a category of people who don't like Monday, I thought, What about Friday? People used to say, "Don't buy a car that was built on Friday," because the autoworkers, according to the story, were too distracted by the approaching weekend to do their best work on Friday.

I happened to know that the woman who looked so good and spoke so well was part of a team at this company that was traveling to a trade show the next week. They were scheduled to leave on Monday.

"How do you feel about traveling on Monday?" I asked her. She would prefer not to, she answered, but she had traveled on Monday before and of course, she would again.

"Have you ever noticed how pilots walk through airports?" I asked. She thought about it for a moment. "Where do you think they teach them to walk like that?" I asked. "Wouldn't you like to go to the school where they teach pilots how to walk? They look so confident, so self-assured."

Do you know why? They have to be. Who would want to get on an airplane with a pilot who trudged through the airport as if he wasn't quite sure where he was going, as *if* it wasn't that important when he got there, or even if he got there? Sometimes you see people walking through airports and the way they are strolling along and looking all around, it seems like they're probably not going to get wherever it is they think they are going. I had a friend who missed a plane one time because he sat down at the wrong gate and didn't realize it until they called the flight -- the plane was going to the right city but it was the wrong airline!

When you have the lives of several hundred people riding on how well you do your job, not most of the time, not nearly every time, but *every single time*, you better walk through the airport like you know where you are going. When people are counting on you, *every time*, you have to walk like it makes a difference if you get there. You have to walk as if you are having a great day and doing a great job.

Who wants to get on a plane with a pilot who looks like he's thinking, "Boy, I hate Mondays. It seems like the weekend will never get here. And it's raining. Today is a day where I could take it or leave it. If things don't go well today, so what? No big loss. I'm in a lousy mood.'"

Forget it! That's not a ride I want to take. Considering this is your life we are talking about, how you hold yourself is vitally important. I'm not talking only about the frame of mind of the person who is flying the plane we are riding on; I'm talking about each of us, because we are flying the plane we're riding on, and the plane is called our lives. My life, and your life. Every day, the quality of your life depends on how you hold yourself, the thoughts you allow yourself to have, and how you look at things.

The fact is, pilots are not the only ones in the *"every single time"* business. What about bankers? How big a difference does it make if they keep proper track of your money? How carefully do you want them to guard your private information? How responsible should the teller be about counting your money, even if he or she is having a rough time on Monday?

What about the mechanic who fixes your brakes? Or the child-care worker taking care of your son or daughter? How about the nurse passing out medications or the radiologist reading an x-ray? Or the bus driver turning a corner in the rain with 40 people on the bus and others in the crosswalk?

The fact is, we are all vitally dependent on one another. Practice the "pilot walk" and see how it affects your confidence. We need each other to do an exceptional job all the time, not just when conditions make it relatively easy. We are all depending on each other, so our need to do an exceptional job is greater than our reluctance to be exceptional, especially since it's Monday.

All the reasons we give ourselves for not providing ECS, I told the woman who asked the "Monday" question, are just a lot of excuses. You don't need them. Your job will be easier and your life will be happier without excuses. Just leave your Funk at the Door and pick it back up when you leave. By leaving your funk at the door, you will see how you can do an exceptional job without it.

How many people did I walk past in the grocery store looking for taco mix before I ran into the manager who offered to drop everything he was doing and show me where it was? Six or seven? A dozen? The store was busy, maybe it was 20? All those people, and I didn't see a single one.

Then suddenly, I was face to face with the manager, looking at his name tag, noticing the color of his hair. Here was someone I would come to know for years and still know today. Suddenly and unexpectedly, we were having a personal experience. Right then and there, without either of us knowing it, I was becoming a loyal customer. It's what I call an "Exceptional Moment of Truth". Exceptional Moments of Truth happen in customer service all the time, but you can't predict them. Part of providing ECS on a consistent basis is always being ready for an Exceptional Moment of Truth.

Something is happening in our world that works in favor of those of us who are committed to providing

ECS all the time. That is, people are becoming hungrier for human connection. One indicator is that, according to the U.S. Census, more people than ever before, 26 percent, are living alone. In fact, there are more people living alone today than there are living in "classic" American families-- a married couple living in a home with at least one child.

When we work in places where we regularly come in contact with other people, there is always the chance to authentically experience someone else. Every time we interact with a human being is a chance to have an Exceptional Moment of Truth.

People want three things from life:

- To be happy

- To be satisfied

- To know their lives make a difference

The first two are by-products of the third one. Having a job gives you the opportunity to create Exceptional Moments of Truth with your customer and your co-workers.

When you are out of work, and spend your days at home, there is a feeling I call, "Waiting for the mail carrier." When I was going through a period like this, without realizing it, I found myself hanging around the front windows at about the time the mail carrier usually arrived.

I was perplexed and one day I asked my mail carrier, "Do people wait for their mail?"

"Yes," he said, "sort of." He explained that in 20 years delivering mail his conclusion was that people who are home alone during the day instinctively don't want to miss what might be their only chance for human contact. Some of them, older people mainly, make no bones about it, he said. They sit by the window and open the door when he arrives. Others, as if by coincidence, happen to be near the door when he comes. "Don't underestimate the power of human connection," he said.

It's valuable to recognize that people are hungry for these Exceptional Moments of Truth. Since these moments of truth are a by-product of providing ECS, we maximize our chances of creating loyal customers when we provide them. Beyond that, we give ourselves that thing which is so sought after. We understand that we make a difference in the lives of others.

Connections With Co-Workers

Every opportunity to interact with a human being is a chance to have a unique moment. Note to self: co-workers are human beings, too.

Sometimes we get so caught up in what we are doing that we forget that all the people around us count, even if they aren't customers. Customers can sense the mood in a place of business, and if the people who work there share an esprit de corps, in other words, a sense of unity, then there is a shared sense of purpose that makes the place more attractive. Even the notion that those who work in a particular place like each other is something that is detectable and powerful. One of the latest retail trends is "scent branding," in which marketers find an aroma that stimulates a particular emotion, such as feelings of power or acquisitiveness, and fill their stores with it. Customers can similarly sense the mood of a place of business. If the people who work there treat the customers one way but treat each other another, doing so indicates inconsistency which is close to dishonesty. The mood of a place, and thus, of a business, is evident in how the people look at one another, the tone of their voices as they speak to each other, their body language and how they move.

Conflicts among co-workers arise, that's a fact, and they most certainly can affect your experience on the job. But if you leave your funk at the door, and you come to work with a frame of mind that has you as ready as you can be to deal with your co-workers as well as your customers, you've got the best chance for creating a winning workplace environment for yourself.

Businesses spend enormous amounts of time and money using psychologists and survey takers to get inside the minds of their customers and prospective customers.

Watch and Listen for Expectations

The lesson behind all this is that you can't deliver what people want if you don't listen to them express their desires. Use this space to answer the following four questions about ECS right now.

- What do you think ECS means?

  _____

  _____

- What does ECS mean to you as a customer?

  _____

  _____

- What does ECS mean to you as someone who provides customer service?

  _____

  _____

- How does ECS feel to you as a customer ?

  _____

  _____

  _____

Read over what you just wrote about ECS. Do you think you can deliver ECS based on your definition of what it means to you? Circle one: YES/ NO

CHALLENGING TIMES FOR DELIVERING ECS

No matter how good you are at delivering ECS, we all face times and circumstances that are challenging. Give short answers to these three questions about challenging times for delivering ECS.

1. How do you respond to the customer who doesn't deserve ECS?

_____

_____

_____

2. What is your solution for "Mondays?"

_____

_____

_____

3. What about if you just don't feel like it?

_____

_____

_____

CUSTOMER EXPECTATIONS

Now let's look at our customers' expectations. Use the space below to answer these three questions about what your customers expect from their experiences with you.

1. What do customers expect? They expect...

   _____

   _____

   _____

2. So...exceeding their expectations looks like what?

   _____

   _____

   _____

3. How could you exceed your customer's expectations?

   _____

   _____

   _____

THE 5 MOST IMPORTANT THINGS TO CUSTOMERS

Now let's take a look at what, over time, customers say are the five most important things that create a great experience for them.

1. **Immediate Attention.** They want to know within a very short time that someone is going to take care of them. It doesn't mean you need to run to them and hop in their lap. Rather, they want to be acknowledged, feel welcome, know their presence is important and that the process of serving them has begun.

2. **A Quality Product.** ECS and a quality product go hand in hand. It is very hard to have one without the other. If you are a bellman at a hotel, your best efforts to escort guests and handle luggage with good manners and efficiency will be sabotaged if you get to the room and the carpet is dirty and the bed is unmade. Consumers have an incredible array of choices today for buying most goods and services, so a quality product is expected. (That's why ECS is often the difference between success and failure.)

3. **To Know You Care.** It makes a huge difference for customers when they know the people who are serving them truly care. Not that you are doing it for the money, although that's part of it. Not that you are providing ECS because you are afraid of what your boss will say, although meeting your boss' approval is a good thing, too. Knowing that the person who is providing them with service is someone who truly cares about them "ranks" on the highest level of importance for customers.

4. **Speed.** We all want to be served in a timely fashion. Every year the way we do business and communicate gets faster. We can perform bank transactions online that just a few years ago, took days. People expect service to happen swiftly. They assume whatever they need can and will be delivered quickly because every other area of their life runs rapidly. Speed is expected.

5. **ECS in Returns.** If they return something, customers don't want to have to wait; they want to be treated with the same great service they would receive if they were buying something for the first time. What happens when you return things?

MOMENTS OF TRUTH
How Satisfied Were You With a Recent Experience?

When you are a customer, how do you evaluate the service you receive? Here's an example. Let's take a look at your satisfaction level as a customer the last time you ate in a restaurant.

Look at the circle on the next page which is divided into eight quadrants. Each quadrant represents an aspect of the service you received:

1. **Initial Greeting**—Were you greeted warmly and promptly with a smile and then seated in a timely fashion?

2. **Atmosphere**—Did the restaurant have a welcoming feeling? Was it decorated? Did it need updating? Was there music playing? Were people having a good time?

3. **Servers**—Were your servers well-dressed, polite, attentive, knowledgeable, and thorough in doing their job? Did they have a smile and seem as if they liked serving you?

4. **Cleanliness**—Was the silverware clean? Were the booths and condiments wiped off? Were the drapes and carpeting clean?

5. **Presentation**—Was the presentation of the food inviting? Was it creative or just thrown on the plate?

6. **Caring Service**—Did you leave with the impression that the host, server and others cared about you and your experience?

7. **Quality of the Meal**—Was the food fresh and hot? Did it taste good and did it meet your expectations?

8. **Final Greeting**—Did someone, when you were leaving, ask if everything was OK and wish you a pleasant evening?

Think about each aspect of service and make a dot in the appropriate section. Depending on how satisfied you were with the service, place the dot closer to the center or to the outside of the circle, with the center representing horrible service and the outside edge representing ECS–customer service that would make you a loyal customer eager to tell others about your great experience.

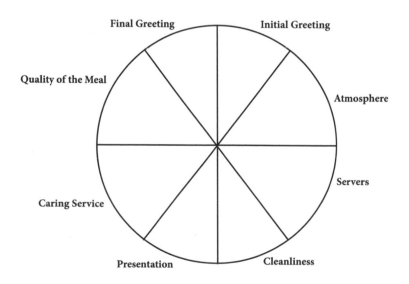

Now answer this question: What do you think you'll remember about your experience at the restaurant, and why? Did the best part of your experience make the strongest impression or was it the worst part? Why do you think it turned out that way?

Place a dot in each quadrant to indicate how satisfied you were with each experience. A dot closest to the center (let's say a 2) is a lower score which indicates a poor customer service experience. A dot in the middle (let's say a 5) indicates a so-so customer experience, and a dot closest to the top (let's say a 9) is a great customer service experience.

Initial Greeting

Final Greeting

Cleanliness

Quality of Meal

Atmosphere

Presentation of Meal

Initial Greeting

Server Caring Service

Now connect the dots. If you received ECS in each of the six areas, you'll have a line that travels around the outside of the circle. The poorer the service you received, the more your line will look like a very tight circle, not reaching out from the center. If your circle looks like a strange star constellation then the service was inconsistent.

How Satisfied Are You With Your Customer Service?

Now think about the job you do. First let's make a list of the eight most important aspects of the service you provide. Use "The 5 Most Important Things to Customers," (use page 106 as a guideline). Think about the timeliness with which you provide service. Are you friendly? Do you treat people like they're special? What is your level of knowledge about your products and services? Do people feel they get value when they interact with you?

Aspects of Service You Provide

1. _____

2. _____

3. _____

4. _____

5. _____

6. _____

7. _____

8. _____

Now, using the circle below, label each sector with one of the aspects of your job. Put dots in each sector according to how effectively you feel you provide customer service in that specific aspect. Draw a line connecting the dots and notice your strengths and weaknesses. Finally, consider these questions: Which aspect of the way you do your job will your customers remember most vividly, and why?

Taking a look at the circle you have drawn by connecting the dots, what are the strongest and weakest points in your performance? First look at the 8-10 dots and when you think about those wonderful

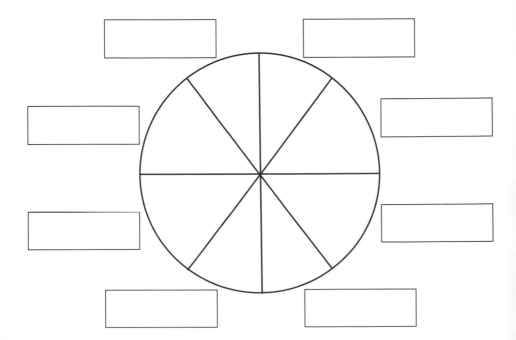

performances which you gave yourself an 8, 9, or 10, stretch out your right arm in front of you, bend it at the elbow, move your head to the right and come across and give yourself a nice pat on the back. Fabulous… nice job!!! Now the not-so-good ones Using the space below, write the three most important things you could do to improve your weak points. If you gave yourself a five in one of the categories, what would you have to do to get to a six? What would you have to do get a seven? Make it fun and really look at how you can improve. (This is an excellent exercise if you are a manager to coach one of your team members).

- Improvement #1

  _____

  _____

- Improvement #2

  _____

  _____

- Improvement #3

  _____

  _____

Employee of the Year

Now let's envision having made those improvements. Imagine winning "Employee of the Year" at your company. Imagine your boss during the awards banquet at your company's annual convention explaining that you've won the award because you've consistently exceeded customers' expectations. Your boss goes on to mention three major ways you have gone above and beyond what your customers expected. List those three great attributes below. Draw on what you learned in the "pie chart" exercise on page 112 and give yourself permission in this private place to list your virtues and finest qualities. Write down three good things your boss says about you!

1. _____

2. _____

3. _____

These are the qualities and abilities you want to recognize in yourself, acknowledge, and build on. One more thing…Felt pretty good winning 'Employee of the Year,' didn't it?

CHAPTER SEVEN

ABOVE AND BEYOND

CREATING LOYALTY THROUGH EXCEPTIONAL MOMENTS OF TRUTH

On Saturday mornings, when there was a line out the door of his Chicago restaurant, Lou Mitchell would walk back and forth on the sidewalk handing small boxes of Milk Duds and donut holes to the women and children. That's one way to greet customers, I thought. The owner shakes your hand and offers you something before you're even inside the front door.

Chicago is a restaurant town. Whether you are looking for the trendiest new cuisine or a deep-dish pizza, there are more choices than you could sample in a lifetime. And like the downtown of any big city, there is a restaurant on just about every corner in which any one of them will serve you a pretty good omelet, a juicy burger, a bowl of hot soup, or a salad. To become legendary, to have people stand outside in the cold waiting to eat at your restaurant, you've got to be exceptional. And Lou Mitchell's family is caring on the tradition.

Lou decided that all the egg orders at his place would be doubled. If you ordered one egg, you got two. If you ordered two, you got four. He served the egg dishes not on plates, but in piping hot skillets carried on wooden platters. Of course, the food was sizzling hot. He served "Texas Toast." It was huge and smothered in butter.

The bacon was as thick as it gets. He served 100% real maple syrup, not a sugary blend. The water for the coffee was triple-filtered and the coffee was so good, he sold you beans to go. Artificial creamers? No way. Every table had a small pitcher of pure cream.

One Saturday morning, my wife Kim and I were standing in line outside Lou Mitchell's on Jackson Boulevard, and I was holding our infant daughter, Stephanie. Lou was passing out Milk Duds and when he came to us, he stopped and looked at Stephanie. He asked if this was her first time at his restaurant, and Kim said, yes.

Lou said "Wait one minute, I have something for you." About a minute later, he returned to the waiting line and took out a 10-dollar bill, gave it to Kim and immediately began apologizing. I mean profusely apologizing. It was one of the most sincere apologies I have ever witnessed, let alone received. He said that in Greece it was the custom to give the parents of a newborn child 10 silver dollars, or the Greek equivalent. The point was the coins had to be silver, but Lou didn't have silver dollars so he was practically begging us to accept the 10-dollar bill with his apologies.

Sometimes restaurant owners can get carried away. Some of them are hams who enjoy having their names on the outside of their places and being the center of attention. People who study the restaurant business sometimes compare it to theater. But there was nothing theatrical about Lou Mitchell's apology to us that day. It was heartfelt and authentic. It was something you couldn't fake.

I'll admit I was a loyal Lou Mitchell's customer already. For some time, I had thought of a trip to Lou Mitchell's as a treat. We didn't live nearby and it wasn't on the way to anyplace, so going to Lou Mitchell's took planning and commitment. Standing outside waiting for a table, holding my infant daughter, was anything but convenient. But the experience was worth it. Then there's Lou and the apology and the $10 bill. How could I not go back? Lou was creating loyal customers over and over just by how he treated us.

This is "An Exceptional Moment of Truth" in customer service. The event took place over 25 years ago and I still can't stop talking about it. Was Lou Mitchell thinking that the moment he was about to create would wind up in a book some day?   No way. He was just being himself, living out his commitment to the way he ran his business.

But I was not the only one who had an Exceptional Moment of Truth at Lou Mitchell's. When I tell this story in a group, it often evokes a similar story from someone else who has experienced Lou Mitchell's, and that's another lesson about the Exceptional Moments of Truth: They feed the positive experiences of others, and in time, they create a sense of agreement among a group of people, a family, a town, or even throughout an industry, that you and/or your business are exceptional at what you do.

Learn this lesson and take it with you throughout your career. Whether you work for different companies or have your own business, the people you come in contact with will tell others how great or not so great you are. Creating the sense that you are exceptional at whatever you do is important, and it will come back to you in ways you cannot imagine. Twenty-one years from now, someone could be raving in a book about something you did, an Exceptional Moment of Truth you created without even knowing it.

Here is another story about an Exceptional Moment of Truth in customer service. My dry cleaner is located one mile from my house. Without thinking about it, I had adopted the business as "my dry cleaner," evidently because it was the closest one to where I live. Like restaurants, there is no shortage of dry cleaners in Chicago. If there is a church, tavern, and a restaurant at a typical intersection, then on the fourth corner is probably a dry cleaner.

Every dry cleaner I've ever used has laundered my shirts. They always come back within one to three days, neatly pressed on hangers. It's as if they all send them out to the same giant factory. With the quality of the product so uniform, your experience dropping off and picking up your clothes can make a big difference.

At my dry cleaner, the TV was always on, tuned to the local news, and even though there never seemed to be anything interesting happening, the proprietor always had half an eye on it. He hated credit cards. The service he used to process transactions was very slow and he complained about it bitterly. Often, it didn't work at all and he had to write down names and card numbers and it just made him angrier. Finally, one December, he announced that after January 1 he wasn't going to take credit cards any more. There was another customer next to me, a huge guy, as big as a football player, and he was dropping off a lot of clothes. "My bill here is usually more than $50," the big guy said. "Sometimes I don't have my checkbook. I usually don't carry that much cash. Credit cards are really convenient...."

I was amazed, but the proprietor cut the man off in mid-sentence. No, he said, it was too slow, it cost too much, and he was getting rid of it. No more credit cards.

I had been going there for five years and never had a problem, but I never went back to the guy again.

A few weeks later, I found a dry cleaner owned and operated by Mr. and Mrs. Cho. Every time I walk through her door she calls out my name in a sing-song voice, "Hellooo, Mister Beck!"

One time she was totaling my bill and it came to a little over $50. "Too much," she said quickly and right there she took off 10 percent. That exceeded my expectations. I'd been going to dry cleaners all my life, and no one had ever taken anything off my bill.

Another time, Mrs. Cho said, "Where is Mrs. Beck today?" Once my wife Kim and I stopped in together, so I was surprised Mrs. Cho remembered my wife.

"Mrs. Beck is working today," I said. "She works at a big company in the accounting department and she is real smart! I work at home, so I get to pick up the dry cleaning."

"No, no, no," Mrs. Cho said. "Mrs. Beck is smart. But you are smarter than Mrs. Beck. You are the smart one." I was shocked.

"How can you say that, Mrs Cho?" I asked.

"Because you married her," she said, and she laughed. I will never forget that Exceptional Moment of Truth.

It solidified my reason why I switched to getting my clothes dry cleaned by Mr. and Mrs. Cho.

Sometimes a seamstress works with Mrs. Cho. She sits at a sewing machine in back. One day, after her customary sing-song, "Helloooo Mister Beck!" Mrs. Cho said, "Yesterday, the sewing lady, you know what she say about you?"

"No," I said. "What did she say?"

"She say you handsome," and then she laughed.

I used to think a dry cleaner is a dry cleaner is a dry cleaner. In five years, I can't remember ever seeing my crabby dry cleaner smile. The only time we spoke more than a few words, he complained about a movie he didn't like. If I ever see Mrs. Cho and she doesn't smile or laugh, I'll assume something is horribly wrong. Where else can I go and in a transaction that lasts less than 3 minutes, here my name sung to me, my wife complimented, and be told I'm handsome and smart?

Mrs. Cho is a perfect combination of consistent ECS, plus the ability to deliver a peak performance. Both are avenues to creating loyal customers who will not only support you for years to come, but will sing your praises louder than any advertising or marketing ever could.

Leave Your Funk at the Door

CHAPTER EIGHT

HAPPINESS

HOW YOUR LOYALTY
CREATES CUSTOMER LOYALTY

Have you ever heard the phrase, "Charity begins at home?" Sir Thomas Browne is credited by some sources as originating the phrase (in 1642) when he wrote, "But how shall we expect charity towards others, when we are uncharitable to ourselves?"

The same thing is true for many qualities, including the loyalty we hope to bring about in our customers. It is hard to get people to give you something you are not willing to give yourself. How can we expect people to be loyal to us if we are not even willing to be loyal to ourselves?

Everyone's heard about America's "Puritan Work Ethic." It's the idea that the road to success is paved with hard work and sacrifice. That's all well and good and no doubt true; however, like all good things, when it goes unchecked, when it's taken to a ridiculous extreme, it can do more harm than good.

Especially in this era, when economic times are tough, it's easy to get down on ourselves and our circumstances and respond by putting our heads down and work ourselves until we drop.

It's a terrible strategy, especially if you plan to grow your career for the long haul.

Taking care of yourself first is important all the time, and crucial when times are hard. As they say before the airplane takes off, "In an emergency, put your own oxygen mask on first before helping others."

I'd like you to create a contract with yourself, a commitment to take care of yourself in such a way that your own satisfaction and happiness is guaranteed. I believe if you nurture and grow these qualities within yourself, they will radiate outward and you will be having great days every day, thus sharing those great days with your customers. After your customers get satisfied, they will become loyal. You will become someone who emanates positive energy into the world, someone who shines, gives off heat and light, and people, including your customers (and your co-workers and bosses), will want to be around you.

Here is a side note you might want to consider in terms of developing your career: Most of us get hired and then work at that business or organization for a period of years. At some point, the job ends or we decide it's time for a change, and we repeat the process hoping to be hired to do a job with more responsibility and more money.

But if you make a commitment to yourself to be at your best every day, you will have an edge that very few people have.

Here are the daily commitments I suggest:

- *Do it for yourself.* Do your job amazingly well, not to please someone else, and certainly not out of fear of losing your job or of being criticized. Do an amazing job every day because what comes out of doing an amazing job is happiness and satisfaction. If you don't believe me, do it for awhile and find out yourself. One possible benefit of doing this amazing job will be that if the layoffs ever happen, your name doesn't even hit the list!

- *Leave your funk at the door.* There will always be excuses and reasons for why today cannot be a great day, and why now is an impossible time to do a great job. This is just the chatter of your mind. Everyone has it, and it's just your funk; it's harmless unless you listen to it. Leave it at the door; it will be right there when you are ready to leave at the end of your workday.

- *Choose to have a great day.* It is within your power to decide beforehand what kind of day it will be. Your experience at your job can be whatever you want it to be, so choose to have a great day every day and see what happens. Before you leave your house in the morning, flip the switch and simply make the choice that things will go smoothly and see what happens. Don't leave something as important as your day to hope. Hoping your day works out turns into hoping your week, month, year and eventually life work out. Your life is too precious to leave up to "hoping it will all work out". Be smart and make your life Great!

- *Affirm your day.* "Today will be a great day all day long." "I will be at my best every moment today." "I have a great intuition and I always know what to say." "I really care about my customers and will assure they get the best service possible." "My customers love doing business with me."

These are affirmations that support your commitment to be at your best all day. Take 2 minutes and verbalize as many as you can every morning before you leave for work. They don't have to be absolutely true; they represent your intentions. You are affirming that these are the qualities you embody and this is how you are declaring you want your day to be.

Our subconscious mind is an incredible tool. I have experienced, and witnessed many people verbalizing and visualizing these affirmations in their lives to achieve things that could have been described as pipe dreams, yet, in some cases within a short period of time, were achieved. Affirmations can go from being "pipe dreams" to being regular parts of our lives.

Affirm your day every day and you will be amazed at how powerful your subconscious mind really is. You will begin to live and feel the day satisfied and happy. This is a story that reminds me of what life is all about and how important attitude plays in our life whenever I read it. Mr. Jones is my hero!

WHEN MR. JONES WAS 92

A 92-year-old man was married for 70 years and his wife had recently passed away. He was too fragile to live by himself anymore and needed to move into an assisted living center. He waited for hours in the lobby..

As he maneuvered his walker into the elevator, on his first day, a staff member told him about his room. The assistant made an enthusiastic attempt to create a positive picture of the room, but the place was not ''top of the line", and no description could hide the fact that the room would be rather meager.

While still on the elevator Mr. Jones said, "I love it," with the enthusiasm of an 8-year-old who'd just been given a new puppy.

"Mr. Jones, you haven't seen it yet," the assistant said. "It's very nice, just wait."

"That doesn't have anything to do with it," Mr. Jones

replied. "Happiness is something you decide on ahead of time," he said. "Whether I like my room or not doesn't depend on how the furniture is arranged...it's how I arrange it in my mind. I already decided to love it.

"It's a decision I make every morning when I wake up. I have a choice: I can spend the day in bed recounting the difficulty I have with the parts of my body that no longer work so well, or I can get out of bed and be thankful for the ones that do.

"Each day is a gift, and as long as my eyes open I'll focus on the new day and all the happy memories I've stored away, just for this time in my life.

"Old age is like a bank account we will all need some day; you withdraw from it what you've put in."

The first lesson from this story is obviously that even when there are plenty of reasons for us to let our funk run us, we can still take control and choose to live happy lives.

The second lesson is that the day will come for each of us when we can no longer do the things we enjoy doing today. The purpose is not that we live out of fear of that day coming, but rather, that we be inspired to live with tremendous energy and intention so that when that day does come, we will be satisfied with our life and in great appreciation for what we have, just like Mr. Jones.

WORDS TO LIVE BY

This is the true joy in life
The being used for a purpose
Recognized by yourself as a mighty one ...
The being a force of Nature
Instead of a feverish selfish little clod
Of ailments and grievances.
Complaining that the world
Will not devote itself
To making you happy.
I am of the opinion that my life
Belongs to the whole community,
And as long as I live,
It is my privilege
To do for it whatever I can.
I want to be thoroughly used up when I die,
For the harder I work, the more I live.
I rejoice in life for its own sake.
Life is no brief candle to me.
It is a sort of splendid torch
Which I've got to hold up for the moment and
I want to make it burn as brightly as possible
Before handing it on to future generations.

— GEORGE BERNARD SHAW

Exceptional Customer Service is not really about the Customer; it's about you. The Customer is the person who receives it! It's really about the person who delivers it and that's you. Want to make a difference in someone's life? Rock their world with some Exceptional Customer Service and you will both win. So keep on being great and until our paths cross again...FIRE UP and Have a Great Day Every Day!

Connecting with customers is top of mind for executives in every industry. Bain & Co. surveys find near-universal agreement among senior managers that improving their company's customer focus is critical for their business success, yet attaining that goal is elusive. "Businesses are losing business they can't afford to lose," according to the results of a recent Harris Poll, which reported 80 percent of customers saying they will never return to a business after a negative customer-service experience.

Bain & Co.'s research has found that while 80% of executives believe that their company delivers outstanding value and a superior customer experience, only 8% of their customers agree. This is a huge discrepancy. This is living in a dream world. This is why I wrote this book and I hope you enjoyed it.

NOTES

LEAVE YOUR FUNK AT THE DOOR

NOTES

LEAVE YOUR FUNK AT THE DOOR